Teacher 2 Teacher

Practical Advice for Educators

Kimberly C. Catlin

WESTBOW
PRESS®
A DIVISION OF THOMAS NELSON
& ZONDERVAN

WestBow Press books may be ordered through booksellers or by contacting:

WestBow Press
A Division of Thomas Nelson & Zondervan
1663 Liberty Drive
Bloomington, IN 47403
www.westbowpress.com
1 (866) 928-1240

ISBN: 978-1-9736-5066-9 (sc)
ISBN: 978-1-9736-5065-2 (e)

Library of Congress Control Number: 2019900335

Print information available on the last page.

WestBow Press rev. date: 01/29/2019

Dedication

I want to give all the glory to my Lord and Savior Jesus Christ.

Acknowledgments

Thanks to my mother, Loretta Bruner for her love and patience.

Thanks to my family, Robert, Alexandra and Rob Jr. for their support.

Thanks to my mentors: Charles and Ruth Beaman, Mary Morton, and William Moody.

Contents

Introduction

So, you've decided to become a teacher. You want to help change the world and make a difference. You like kids and would enjoy a long summer vacation. You have a lot to offer and think it would be fun. After all, how hard can it be, right? Wrong. Most teachers had the same idea when they began. After all the test, course work and field work, money spent and hours of planning, you feel prepared. The only problem is, everything changes when you actually enter your classroom and begin your job. That is when the rubber hits the road and reality sets in.

You can do it and will accomplish everything you have planned. If you need a little advice along the way, I have comprised a detailed collection of advice. It is for those new to the profession as well as seasoned professionals and is designed for individuals or groups. As you read, note adjustments that you can make to fit your particular situation or area of need. Remember, this is advice. Take it or leave it. It is written in plain, uncomplicated words. I have included every possible thing that you might need to know to help you succeed from the first day you enter the classroom until the day you retire. Now, take a deep breath and jump on in!

Your Job

1. You are responsible for all the children in your school until they leave the school grounds.

2. Yes, there will be days when you will wonder why you ever wanted to teach.

3. Don't drown in paperwork. Prioritize!

4. Teachers need to be committed to the welfare and education of children.

5. Keep everything legal. Legalities work for and against you.

6. Come early or stay late to avoid taking work home.

7. Change schools if you need a change.

8. Change subjects if you need a change.

9. Change grades if you need a change.

10. Document. Document, document! It is worth the time it takes.

11. Always arrive a few minutes early for work, meetings, etc.

12. Call if you know you will be late. Someone has to cover your class for you.

13. Protect the children.

14. Without haste, report suspicious evidence and behavior to the proper authorities.

15. Don't believe everything you are told, see or read.

16. Make yourself a valuable employee.

17. Join the local teacher's union.

18. Know your legal rights and responsibilities.

19. From time to time, attend workshops. They can be refreshing and informative.

20. Take threats seriously. It could save a life.

21. If a child complains of a stomach ache, have them go to the restroom. If it persist or gets worse, call a parent. Also know and keep your eyes open for signs of abuse.

22. Keep accurate records.

23. Check your mailbox and email more than once a day.

24. Take notes at faculty meetings, team meetings and parent conferences. Don't rely on you memory or someone else.

25. Take care of personal business on your own time and expect it of others as well.

26. Find and keep good substitute teachers.

27. Investigate all angles before making a decision.

28. Avoid breaking up fights. Warn verbally and send for an administrator or SRO. Students should not be encouraged to help break up fights. Someone might get hurt and you are liable. But if you have no choice, intervene and break it up.

29. Report all accidents and injuries as soon as possible.

30. It is a good idea to keep a file on each student.

31. Learn as much about management as you can because it will be 90% of your job.

32. Keep inventory of all your equipment.

33. There will be days when you will have to take on extra duties. Handle it with stride.

34. Don't stand around talking when you should be working.

35. Don't make excuses for yourself. Handle your business.

36. Prepare a sub folder before the end of the first week of school. You never know what will happen.

37. Keep enough basic, extra work to last a few weeks.

38. Always review everything you will show to your students.

39. Limit your personal visitors. You are there to work.

40. Volunteer your time to tutor students that are struggling. It is worth it.

41. Go to work, do your job, go home.

42. Select another profession if you are seeking monetary wealth.

43. Never miss deadlines! You could throw a lot of things out of whack.

44. Train students for drills (fire, tornado, security, etc.) before they occur. No matter what age you teach, reassure them that they will be safe.

45. Review student records and information. It will help you help them.

46. Follow all federal and state laws.

47. By law, you must make accommodations for special needs and disabled students.

48. Keep all exterior doors and windows locked. Teach students to never open them.

49. Make sure all classroom visitors check in at the main office.

50. Never allow strangers near the children.

51. Count your students coming and going while outside of the building. They sometimes stray.

52. If you know there is a sub in the building, offer your help.

53. Display student work and tell them how wonderful it looks.

54. Never disclose personal information about your students to anyone.

55. Never display photographs or images of students to anyone without written permission from parents, especially on social media.

56. No matter what age, teach them to line up. It is a part of life.

57. Make sure to have agreements in writing and preferable with a witness.

58. Keep a record of who a child can and cannot be released to with proper identification and always through the main office.

59. Use translators when needed.

60. If you have a guest speaker, be sure to know exactly what they will say or show to your class.

61. Have a third person present when dealing with an angry parent, co-worker or student.

62. Stay on schedule!

63. If you realize teaching just isn't your thing, get out now.

64. If it isn't your responsibility, don't complain.

65. Repeat, repeat, repeat.

66. Always double check attendance records (Tardies, absences, early dismissals, suspensions, etc.) Your records may be used in a court of law.

67. Save excuse notes.

68. Beware of the media! They have a knack for misquoting.

69. Confront strangers that do not have a visitors pass.

70. Know specifically what your job is and isn't.

71. Medication (prescription and non-prescription) should be kept in the office.

72. Only parents or specific personnel should administer medication to students.

73. Teach a subject unfamiliar to you. You grow from trying new things.

74. If you don't get along with one of your co-workers, parents, boss, etc. don't let your students see or hear your negative attitude.

75. Remove or resolve problems and distractions quickly so that you don't waste instructional time.

76. You should be entitled to a duty free lunch period.

77. Never sign anything before reading it first.

78. Never "gang up" on a student.

79. Never discriminate because of race, gender, ethnicity, personal belief system or religion, etc. Your job is to teach everyone in your class.

80. Follow due process procedures.

81. Invite guest speakers. Your class needs to see a fresh face and different perspective from time to time.

82. Keep website information up to date.

Robert Catlin Jr.

7

Your Lessons

1. Keep lesson plans but understand that they are not carved in stone. Roll with it!

2. Teach your students how to act when you are absent.

3. Be spontaneous! It will keep your students on the edge of their seats!

4. Show respect and interest in cultures other than your own. You will learn so much!

5. Teach your students to respect the flag and what it stands for.

6. Teach your students to apologize. Humility is a virtue.

7. Teach your students the art of good conversation. Present interesting conversation starts. Don't allow one person to "hog" the conversation or anyone to be overlooked.

8. Develop a signal system (bells, whistle, etc.) to get attention. Save your voice!

9. Teach responsibility and accountability.

10. Teach and model good manners.

11. Teach students to respect boundaries and personal space.

12. Adjust lessons to fit student learning.

13. Teach stranger danger no matter what age group you teach.

14. Teach your class to be quiet when silence is essential.

15. Teach your students to submit to authority. This is a life lesson.

16. Use whatever you have to help your students understand what you are trying to teach them.

17. Make real life connections at every opportunity!

18. Teach your students to love reading!

19. Keep things moving at a steady and manageable pace.

20. Teach your students to respect themselves and others.

21. Teach independence!

22. Teach until your students "get it". Regardless of how long it takes.

23. Take a break from difficult lessons but revisit them.

24. Teach students to question, reason and research.

25. Timing is important, so be mindful of when you plan events and lessons.

26. Teach and practice self-control.

27. It is a good idea to have quiet time for your class. To rest, reflect or rejuvenate. They will realize you are human.

28. Know the definition of vandalism and teach it to your students.

29. Teach your students the value of a good education without making them feel that you need to attend college to be successful.

30. Teach students to love themselves!

31. Help students find a good role model/hero.

32. Help students understand that the lives of celebrities are not the same lives as average people. Fame and fortune aren't everything.

33. Teach students that television and movies are make-believe and not real.

34. Teach students to become good losers because they will lose more often than win.

35. Incorporate current events in your lessons whenever you have the opportunity but use good judgement.

36. You never really know a subject until you teach it to someone else!

37. Introduce, teach, review.

You

1. Use common sense.

2. Rise above pettiness.

3. You will be around children all day, every day, for years.

4. You will be taken for granted.

5. Everyone remembers their best and worst teacher and why.

6. Let it go! Don't be revengeful.

7. Join the local sick bank. You don't know what the future has in store.

8. Learn more than one route to school and make sure your family knows your routine route.

9. Embarrassment can be humbling.

10. Your hearing, memory and vision will worsen with age, which is not always a bad thing.

11. Never underestimate always overestimate.

12. You will learn more during difficult times.

13.   Don't magnify small problems.

14.   Never say never! You may end up eating your words.

15.   If you embarrass yourself, acknowledge it and move on.

16.   Love must be generously given away on a daily basis.

17.   Respect must be earned and can be lost in a matter of minutes.

18.   Be diligent and determined.

19.   Don't paint yourself into a corner!

20.   Draw a line between your personal and professional life.

21.   Avoid power struggles.

22.   Reward yourself on paydays!

23.   Step inside their world, but don't stay there.

24.   If it looks and acts like a snake, it's a snake.

25.   Keep your promises. Children have good memories.

26.   Avoid eating home baked goods if you are concerned with hygiene, storage at correct temperatures, and ingredients. Say "thanks, I'll eat it later".

27.   You know what they say about assumptions!

28.   Video tape yourself teaching. You will be surprised at what you see.

29.   A reason is not the same thing as an excuse.

30. Allow gum only if you are prepared to find it on furniture, floors and in hair. Not to mention popping, sharing and smacking during your lesson.

31. Don't keep anything that triggers an allergic reaction in others. Ask about the common allergens: latex, wheat, peanuts but some people have rare and life threatening ones.

32. Learn to recognize the signs of seizure, stroke, choking, heart attack and asthma.

33. Have sugar-free sweets available so that no one feels left out.

34. Keep peppermints available. They open stuffed noses, settle upset stomachs, and sooth sore throats, but avoid allowing students to bring candy. Also, be mindful of the age of the student. If they choke, you are liable.

35. Walk the walk.

36. Assert authority not superiority.

37. You will have to raise your voice from time to time. Use it effectively and sparingly. Avoid yelling at a student, especially if you are angry.

38. Over the years you will develop frown lines between your eyes!

39. Stand on your head if it will get their attention!

40. Whoever said "It takes a village" knew what they were talking about. You simply cannot go it alone.

41. Take a day or half-day off just because you can.

42. Adjust their attitude, and yours, if needed.

43. After about 15 years, you will have to find your second wind!

44. Feel free to vent but make sure it is at the proper time and to someone who cares and will understand.

45. Avoid drinking (coffee, water, etc.) in class, if you must, never leave your drink unattended.

46. Times change, people don't.

47. Never allow sexual advances.

48. Leave your pets at home. Law suit!

49. Sometimes a good comeback is necessary.

50. Count your blessings!

51. Accept criticism, but consider the source.

52. Criticize with care.

53. Watch your body language. Use it to your advantage.

54. Keep an open mind.

55. Halloween, April Fool's Day and Valentine's Day can be a pain in the neck.

56. Practice controlling your emotions.

57. Stay focused!

58. Have a personal vision and goal.

59. Learn from your students.

60. Embrace diversity!

61. Get out of the building! Field trips can be an exciting and memorable learning experience.

62. Find a mentor, be a mentor.

63. Keep things simple and uncomplicated.

64. Have a plan!

65. Avoid complaining. Things could always we worse. If you must complain, complain to your dog.

66. Strive to become a team player.

67. Give credit where credit is due!

68. Stand your ground.

69. Don't do or say anything that could land you in court before a judge.

70. Think with the outcome in mind or you may wish you had.

71. Avoid judgements.

72. Keep hard copies of important stuff. Remember, computers crash.

73. Never tolerate insubordination.

74. Empathize.

75. You will come to value peace and quiet.

76. It may take years for you to see the fruits of your labor yield gains, but you will.

77. Keep your vocabulary at grade level, but introduce new words.

78. Routine, routine, routine.

79. Take care of problems as soon as they arise.

80. You'll have to teach when you are tired, hungry and uncomfortable.

81. They will have to learn when they are tired, hungry and uncomfortable.

82. Learn to laugh at yourself!

83. Be careful what you do in your private life. Social media is not only an open book, but it is permanent.

84. Don't go to work if you are sick. You will only be a burden to everyone.

85. You don't have to take on every opportunity that presents itself. It is okay to say "No".

86. Watch teacher movies!

87. If your school sells yearbooks, purchase one each year. You will be surprised at how quickly things change.

88. Foster their imagination!!!!!

89. Don't allow your pride to get in the way of good judgement.

90. Avoid taking hurtful comments personally, even if they are meant to hurt. In other words, guard your heart.

91. Trust your instincts.

92. Understand that you will change throughout the years.

93. Keep your keys in your pocket or around your neck. If you put them down, they may disappear.

94. Subscribe to at least one educational magazine or website.

95. Have an after school reward planned when your day is long or difficult.

96. Have photos of your last vacation, wedding, family, pets, etc. Post them in your classroom.

97. Some days will be tough as nails, push through them.

98. Some days you will not be in a good mood. Fake it.

99. Sometimes you have to look the other way but use good judgement.

100. Relay the message "We are having school".

101. Little ears. Big mouths.

102. Allow students to "overhear" you saying positive things about them.

103. Take advice from those that are wise. Avoid fools and every type of idiot.

104. Watch for teachable moments.

105. Explain "zero tolerance" and what it includes.

106. Learn to deal with difficult people.

107. You will get better each day.

108. Be consistent!

109. Teach with purpose!

110. Forgive. Yourself and others.

111. Mean what you say and say what you mean. You will lose all credibility otherwise.

112. Make a big deal over gifts, no matter how small.

113. Always give fair warning before you take action.

114. Lessons sometimes have to learned the hard way.

115. As the years pass, you will be a guest at weddings, visit hospitals and attend funerals.

116. Perfect your "poker face".

117. Practice tough love.

118. Find a good masseuse, doctor and chiropractor. Teaching is a stressful job.

119. Don't create your own problems.

120. Act wacky! It is a great stress reliever for you and your students.

121. Learn to deal with drama.

122. Defuse situations before they erupt.

123. Use caution and compassion when dealing with gender related issues.

124. Don't beat yourself up if you make a mistake. Try to fix it, learn from it, and never do it again.

125. Prepare yourself for a life of service.

126. Work on your weaknesses and value your strengths.

127. Embrace challenges!

128. Get to work early from time to time. Relax, play music, sip a cup of coffee and ease into your day.

129. Bite your tongue, especially if profanity is on the tip of it.

130. If you don't bend, you might break.

131. Draw the line and deal with the first person that crosses it. Make an example of them, without being harsh or sarcastic. The punishment should fit the crime. Then everyone will know you mean business.

132. Take control of your classroom from day one.

133. Get rid of unnecessary baggage.

134. Always, always, always have a back-up plan!

135. Snow days are bliss!

136. Understand that children sometimes cannot find the words to say what they are thinking or feeling.

137. Enjoy the journey. Mark the years. Make memories.

138. Don't expect your non-teacher friends/family to understand what you encounter on a day to day basis.

139. You will be tired at the end of the day.

140. Learn the language, slang and lingo of the age group you are teaching.

141. Attitude is everything.

142. Some things will become easier as you age, while others will become more difficult.

143. Remember, you are the authority in your classroom. Don't try to be one of their peers.

144. Try to leave the job at the job.

145. Ask for help if you need it.

146. Take each day as it comes.

147. It is okay to cry.

148. Keep a sense of humor.

149. Females: Beware of short skirts, low tops, tight or see through clothing as well as bracelets that can get hung on clothes. High heels may be cute but your feet will ache at the end of the day, besides, you cannot run in heels.

150. Males: Beware of tight clothes and open shirts as well as your roaming eyes.

151. Dress professionally, but comfortably.

152. Be proactive and avoid being reactive.

153. Walk away if you feel your temper rising or you feel that you are in danger.

154. Enforce the rules. Otherwise it is a waste of time having them.

155. ALWAYS do the right thing even if you are alone in doing so!

156. Never betray a trust.

157. Never cross the line!

158. Let your students see pictures of you at their age. It will delight them!

159. Always be professional.

160. Always be respectful to everyone.

161. Take care of your health. Take vitamin C beginning a week before school starts.

162. Learn to ignore little things. In other words, pick your battles.

163. Keep valuables at home. If you must bring valuables, lock them up. Keep cell phones in your pocket. The moment you put it down and turn your back, someone will pick it up.

164. Start a home reference library collection.

165. Read books about education from a variety of sources and points of view.

166. Remember the type of child you were!

167. Eat when you need to eat and eat well. You will need the energy.

168. Remember what you learned in psychology class. You'll need it!

169. Rest when you need to rest.

170. Embrace change. Make it your best friend because it will be your constant companion.

171. Practice patience. This one thing can save your sanity.

172. Listen with an open heart and a closed mouth.

173. Instead of complaining about what your students cannot do, help them do what they can do.

174. If you don't love children (yeah, love), you will not last in this profession.

175. Seriously consider why you want to teach. Make a list of pros and cons.

176. Don't compromise your values.

177. Live a balanced life!

178. Realize it takes time to learn how to teach. Hit and miss.

179. Be the adult, even when you want to throw a tantrum!

180. You are responsible for all your actions and behaviors and teach your students that they are as well.

181. Everything you have ever experienced was for such a time as this.

182. Never think you've seen it all, because you haven't!

183. Never think you know it all, because you don't!

184. Ask questions. You are learning as well.

185. Apologize when you are at fault.

186. Enjoy your job. Have fun!

187. Beware of your thoughts, they can become words. Beware your words, they can become actions.

188. Keep a calendar.

189. Never say anything you cannot back up or enforce.

190. Read Blooms Revised Taxonomy.

191. Read to your students, no matter what age, and have them read to you and others. Avoid making a student real aloud if they don't want to.

192. Examine your check stub.

193. Beware of home visits. You are on your own.

194. Negativity is contagious.

195. Don't react to everything good or bad. A stone face is more effective than you can imagine!

196. Avoid getting tangled up in the personal lives of your students. Be involved, but keep your distance.

197. Teach, practice and demonstrate cooperation and team building.

198. Keep extra umbrellas!

199. No pity parties! At least you have a job and a long vacation.

200. Never accuse without solid evidence.

201. Everyone has problems.

202. Never backstab or throw anyone under the bus. It always comes back on you.

203. Avoid skipping breakfast or lunch. You'll be grumpy by the afternoon.

204. Teach until the last day of school, especially before breaks, to send the message that school is school. It will cut your discipline problems in half.

205. Do YOUR homework!

206. Don't burn your bridges.

207. For luncheons, it is a good idea to bring your dish in an aluminum pan. No clean up.

208. Don't be a parasite.

209. Outstanding tattoos, nose rings, weird hair and make-up are all unprofessional.

210. Perfect the art negotiation.

211. Miracles will happen.

212. Accept the fact that some things are beyond your control.

213. It is not what you say as much as it is how you say it.

214. Use all your senses.

215. Hearing from former students is the best reward of all!

216. There will be times when you must throw your hands up and surrender. It's okay.

217. Get students to line up by holding your hand over each child as you walk down the line. Works every time!

218. Have a term you can use to re-direct conversation/behavior. It will turn the tide.

219. Vomiting can cause a chain reaction!

220. Frustration is normal.

221. Avoid assigning extra work as punishment.

222. Make homework meaningful to re-enforce lessons. Anything else is a waste of time.

223. Remember, our behaviors are shaped by our emotions.

224. Have interesting things for early finishers to do.

225. It takes 30 days to break or start a habit

226. Everyone has a story.

227. Be a peacemaker, not a troublemaker.

228. Cheaters never prosper? Sometimes they do, but they usually get caught.

229. Never verbally abuse a student. Never give physical punishment.

230. Remember, you cannot make anyone do anything. You cannot get around free will.

231. Bury the past.

232. Don't expect perfection. We are all human.

233. You will encounter crazy folks!

234. Don't be a tattle-tale.

235. Pay attention to details.

236. Cover your-bases.

237. Use controversy to your advantage.

238. Take a self-defense class. Teacher assaults are on the rise.

239. You will learn to think on your feet.

240. Test and data run the show.

241. The playing field is never level.

242. Children (and adults) will ask you anything, anytime, anywhere.

243. Avoid every kind of trap.

244. Have a bag of tricks!

245. Over the years, you will see the future pass before your eyes.

246. Never allow behavior to be a factor in grading. Grade with fairness.

247. Even if your students tower over you, they are still children.

248. You will be a tiny footnote in the life of each student. Use that small window of opportunity.

249. As the years pass, you will become desensitized to some issues but do not allow your heart to become hard.

250. Teach tolerance.

251. You will adjust to high levels of noise.

252. Gangs are real and dangerous. Learn the signs of gang activity.

253. Don't be naïve about the truths concerning sex, drugs, etc. between students, co-workers and parents.

254. You will encounter so many different personalities!

255. Handle melt downs with tact. Your and theirs.

256. Be conscience of your behavior in public places.

257. Leave for the day as if you will not return. You may not.

258. Walk a few miles in someone else shoes.

259. Remember, you are fighting against the distractions of the world.

260. Understand that YOU might be the problem.

261. You will be inundated with surveys, rules, procedures, programs, requirements, meetings, emails, etc. It is all part of the job.

262. Before you give up, take a look at the want ads and obituaries. It might make you think again.

263. You will see things that are disturbing, hear things that are unbelievable, and smell things that will make you gag.

264. Never say anything to a student that you would not say in the presence of their parents.

265. Don't expect your students to follow rules if you don't.

266. If you are not authorized to do or say something, don't do it.

267. In other words, stay in your place.

Your students

1. Prepare your students for the future, even if they resist or don't understand.

2. Never allow your students to address you in any way other than formally.

3. NEVER take advantage of the innocence of a child!

4. Things that may seem silly, minor or insignificant to us, may be a big deal to them.

5. Remember, they are children, not little adults.

6. Your #1 prior is the children!

7. Begin training your students from day one.

8. Learn names as soon as possible.

9. Don't neglect the average kids that seem to blend into the background.

10. Never be alone in a room with a student with the door closed.

11. Never touch a student except to give a pat on the back, side hug or fist bump.

12. Learn your students. Spend time with each one.

13. Never leave a class unattended.

14. Guard your words; they will stay with your students forever.

15. Don't allow bullying. Explain the seriousness and possible consequences.

16. Know the average attention span of the age group you are teaching.

17. Never take money from students unless it is for a specific purpose and always use a collection log. Follow your district policy on these types of issues.

18. Celebrate accomplishments, no matter how small.

19. Your students will tell everything that goes on in your classroom, the good, the bad and the ugly!

20. Be honest with your students. They will not trust you if they catch you in a lie.

21. If you suspect a student is hiding contraband items get the proper authorities to handle it.

22. Never leave a student unattended in your classroom.

23. Never leave two students in your classroom unattended.

24. Never allow the dozens, burning, or any form of verbal abuse. It may start out as fun but may end in an altercation.

25. Don't allow students to bring toys, expensive gifts, etc. It is distracting and will cause problems if lost, stolen or broken.

26. Remember, children do what they are allowed to do.

27. Mourn with a student that is in mourning.

28. Celebrate with a student that has something to celebrate.

29. Cry with your students when they need to cry.

30. Laugh with them even if their jokes are not funny but never laugh at them.

31. Give them hope, not pity.

32. Remember, the class clown might be rich and famous one day.

33. Meet each student where they are and lead them where they need to be.

34. You will lose some students to drugs, violence and death. Just watch the news.

35. Remember, the reasoning part of their brain isn't fully developed yet, but yours is.

36. Beware of the quiet ones. You don't know what they are thinking, while the loud ones tell you everything on their minds.

37. Watch for sudden and/or severe changes in behavior. There could be a hidden problem.

38. Give that student that just has to have attention a job to do.

39. To some of your students, school is the only place they feel safe and cared for.

40. Avoid embarrassing a student.

41. Teach your students how to think not what to think.

42. Teach your students that fair is not the same as equal.

43. By law, you must report abuse.

44. Encourage students to stay at home if they are ill. No sense in everyone getting sick.

45. Avoid eating in front of students in class. You will look unprofessional and they might beg for food.

46. Focus on what is in the best interest of the students, not you.

47. Believe in them and believe in yourself.

48. Your students are always watching you.

49. Send students to the office after you have exhausted every attempt to re-direct their negative behavior.

50. Avoid mass punishments and mass rewards.

51. Each student has their own learning style. Find out what it is and teach them how to use it to their advantage.

52. Children are usually a reflection of their upbringing.

53. There is nothing wrong with a little healthy competition.

54. Let your students know that you are the boss of your classroom.

55. Do not give a student your responsibilities, such as taking attendance or entering grades on your computer.

56. Help your students set and reach goals (short and long term).

57. Changes in circumstances create changes in behavior.

58. Children get just as excited about breaks as teachers do.

59. There is something to be said about the phase of the moon. Hmmm

60. Boys will be boys! Think about it.

61. Girls talk, usually about boys and one another. Nip it if it gets ugly and out of hand.

62. Never give a student a ride without the verbal or written consent of the parent. You are liable.

63. Make your students feel that they can do the impossible!

64. Don't compare siblings.

65. Don't wait until a student is out of control before you take action. Call home, send a note, or schedule a conference.

66. Do not allow students to act the way they act at home if it is unacceptable.

67. Make new students feel welcome and give them time to adjust and fit in.

68. From time to time, eat lunch with your students.

69. To your students, you seem old. Use it to your advantage.

70. Remember to ask about the new baby, lost dog, etc. It is all about relationships!

71. Remain neutral in the area of sensitive subjects and situations.

72. Calm their fears. There is a reason why they are afraid.

73. Yes, there is a child worse than the one you have in class.

74. Know the medical information on your students.

75. Realize anyone that will be with your students on field trips and activities must (in most school systems) have a background check.

76. Do not allow students to video or photograph you or others.

77. Avoid labeling students.

78. Never allow students to touch you inappropriately, comb your hair, kiss you, massage your neck, sit on your lap, or eat after you. Use good judgement.

79. Remember, your students must deal with their peers, pressure and all.

80. That bad student gets on everyone's nerves, not just yours.

81. Don't allow students to talk negatively about co-workers and administration, even if they are right.

82. You don't have to like every student you have in class but you are being paid to teach them. Find something to like about them.

83. Find a way to reach each student.

84. Sometimes you need to leave a student alone and let things work themselves out, especially with middle school age children, but let them know you are available.

85. Tweens are called tweens for a reason!

86. You must work with your students individually and as a group and they must learn to do the same.

87. If you want to see yourself, watch your students interacting.

88. You will have some classes that are a total nightmare!

89. That "problem child" is never sick.

90. You will have students that will simply melt your heart!

91. Always allow your students to save face, especially older students.

92. Keep your eyes open, especially during springtime. Boys and girls do more than flirt.

93. Never treat a student badly because you don't like them, their parents or their sibling.

94. Instead of complaining about the student that keeps falling asleep in class, find out why.

95. Never discus your personal views on religion or politics with your class. If they ask a question, answer it honestly and professionally or don't answer it at all. Review the law on this issue.

96. Don't demand your students look you in the eye. Their ears still work.

97. Peer tutoring is a valuable learning tool.

98. Acquire as much knowledge of special needs students as you can.

99. Avoid going to the restroom with children. Children must learn to fasten their own pants.

100. Give second chances.

101. Natural born talkers are natural born talkers!

102. Keep tight reins on that problem child!

103. Gently try to draw that quiet, shy one out of their shell and help them soar!

104. Never tell a student that they are stupid, worthless, odd, etc.

105. Avoid sending a troublemaker in the hall to wait for you to reprimand them. Unsupervised and angry are a bad combination. Call for help, wait until after class, or place the child another area.

106. Never send a student anywhere without a hall pass.

107. Avoid holding a student in your class if they should be elsewhere. Call or send a note.

108. Group students in ways that will help them learn to work together.

109. If you cannot pronounce a student's name, ask, and then write it down in a way that you can remember how to say it.

110. Nicknames are okay as long as they are appropriate and not offensive.

111. Make sure new students know how they will get home before dismissal time.

112. Yeah, it is weird for your students to see you outside of the classroom setting.

113. Make sure the punishment fits the crime.

114. Know the difference between discipline and punishment.

115. Reprimand privately.

116. Never give up on a child.

117. Times of transition are when most problems occur.

118. Insecurity can show itself in a variety of ways.

119. Don't be shocked if you are referred to (verbally or in writing) in a derogatory or profane way or personally insulted. Unless it is a threat, let it go.

120. Never refuse to sign a yearbook or display a drawing.

121. Never allow anyone to feel weird, stupid or out of place.

122. Belittling is a no-no.

123. Don't show favorites, even if you have one.

124. Avoid bribing students to get them to behave or do their work. It always backfires. Teach them to earn what they receive.

125. It is okay to spoil your students, but don't make it a habit.

126. Learn to discern if a student needs to go to the restroom or just wants to get out of class.

127. Be confident. Students can smell fear.

128. Make sure your students know what an emergency is and isn't.

Your Parents

1. Get back to parents as quickly as possible.

2. Be gentle with parents.

3. Invite parents to your classroom.

4. Make sure you have updated parent contact information.

5. After you have children, you will know how parents feel.

6. Help parents help their children.

7. Work with parents and encourage them to work with you.

8. Parents will protest against some of the rules, but stand your ground and remain professional.

9. If parents become too much of a problem, consult your principal.

10. Seize every opportunity to meet parents. They need to see your face and you need to see theirs.

11. Avoid offering your personal views on child rearing.

12. Parents should schedule a time to meet with you. Guard your time.

13. Sometimes parents don't know what to do.

14. Sometimes parents expect you to do everything for their children.

15. Sometimes parents are in denial.

16. Sometimes parents cannot see that they are the problem.

17. Don't listen when a parent says "Just threat them like you would your own child" or "spank them". Even if they put it in writing. Don't do it!

18. Parents should make you aware of medications their child is taking, what it is for, and the side effects.

19. Most parents think their child is the most important.

20. Never argue with a parent, especially in the presence of students.

21. Help parents with contacts that will help them and their child.

22. Never tell a student that something their parent is teaching them is wrong or stupid, even if it is. If it is a serious issue, direct them to the guidance office or allow them the opportunity to discover the truth on their own.

23. Regularly inform parents about your class through notes, email, webpage, call outs, etc.

Your Co-Workers

1. Get to know your co-workers.

2. Avoid gossip!

3. Avoid fraternizing with co-workers.

4. Visit classrooms of co-workers you admire and take notes.

5. Share helpful information.

6. Celebrate retirements. It will be your turn one day.

7. If you need something but cannot leave your class, send a reliable student with a note to a co-worker.

8. Make a deal with a co-worker to "babysit" your problem child and vice versa.

9. Support your co-workers, they will be your second family.

10. Find someone at work that you can trust.

11. Whenever you're dealing with money, have a co-worker check your figures, especially if the amount is large.

12. It is a good idea to have personal contact information of selected co-workers.

13. Fine out who lives nearby, you might need a ride one day.

14. You don't have to like everyone you work with, but you do have to work with them.

15. Never feel that you are more important than someone else. You're not.

16. Co-workers include everyone, not just teachers.

17. Over the years you will make so many wonderful friendships that will last for years.

18. Support one another-always have someone's back!

19. Congratulate the Teacher of the Year though you think it should have been you.

20. You will work with a know-it-all!

21. You will work with a whiner!

22. You will work with a super teacher.

23. You will work with a slacker.

24. Never usurp a co-workers authority. Agree, ignore or stand there in silence.

25. No one likes a tattle tale.

26. Yes, there will be clicks.

27. Get to know part-time, support staff, cafeteria workers and custodians.

28. Hug someone that is having a bad day.

29. Sometimes a student just needs a walk. Make an agreement with a co-worker that is you send a student with a note that says "JNAW", allow them to chill out a minute before they return to your class. Act like the note is legit.

30. You are all on the same team, act like it.

31. Be respectful with others time.

32. Pay attention in meetings, contribute to the task and avoid being rude.

33. Carry you weight and don't expect others to carry it for you.

34. Use caution when borrowing or lending.

35. No matter what you do, everyone will not like you. There will be haters. That's life!

36. No matter how long you have been teaching, never forget how it feels to be new to the profession. Help others.

37. If you know someone is in violation of the law, especially if it hurts a child, confront them ASAP.

38. Cry together. Laugh together. Dream the impossible together.

39. The most important people in the building are the secretaries custodians, and support staff. You cannot run a school without them.

40. One thank you can go a long way!

41. You do you.

47

Your Administrators and Central Office/BOE

1. Avoid giving your opinion unless it is specifically asked for.

2. Know when to speak up and when to shut up.

3. Your boss is under more pressure than you will ever know.

4. Know when to back down and when to stand your ground.

5. Invite your principal to your class and have them participate.

6. Avoid the political side of the job, if you can.

7. Begin planning for retirement as soon as the ink is dry on your contract!

8. Read your contract and your educational agreement.

9. Save your clean receipts. Your bookkeeper will need them.

10. Know all the policies and procedures for your school and district.

11. Feel free to question your evaluation, assignment, etc.

12. Avoid bad mouthing your boss.

13. The principal sets the tone for the school.

14. Ask and you may receive, don't ask and you get nothing.

15. Get permission and clearance before you order anything, or you may end up paying for it yourself.

16. New programs come and go and come and go and come....

17. If it is against your personal belief, don't do it.

18. Know the policy for inclement weather and emergencies before you are faced with it.

19. Make sure the main office has your personal and medical information and contacts.

20. If you go to the principal with a problem, have a few suggestions for solutions.

21. You can refuse certain duties. Check your educational agreement and contract

22. Review your personal file every few years to make sure it is accurate.

23. License requirements differ from state to state.

24. You won't be paid what you are worth.

25. Keep up to date on board meeting agenda and outcomes.

26. Utilize funds set aside for your use.

27. Voice your opinion in matters that will affect you.

28. Don't think that you cannot lose your job. Roles, rules and demands change frequently.

29. Be informed of your benefits and take advantage of each one.

30. Get used to acronyms!

31. Your boss isn't your buddy.

32. Don't brown-nose, suck up or kiss up to your boss. Just do your job the best you can.

Your Classroom

1. Get and stay organized.

2. Make your workplace comfortable (you will live there!)

3. Decide on your class rules with student input. Post them and review /refer to them when needed.

4. Keep your classroom clean.

5. Keep some of your favorite things at work (candy, drinks, etc.) for those days when you miss lunch or need and afternoon boost.

6. Keep a ball, jump rope, or anything that you can play with outdoors.

7. Assign classroom duties and have them rotate jobs so that everyone gets a change to participate.

8. Keep extra clothes for your students. Visit a second hand store.

9. Keep adhesive bandages but never apply them.

10. Keep a few personal items at work. (comb, breath mints, etc.)

11. Keep extra supplies for students and co-workers. Let's make a deal!

12. Keep extra clothes/shoes at work. You never know if you will need them.

13. Have a flashlight, small set of tools and sewing kit on hand.

14. Keep tissues and hand sanitizers within reach, especially during the winter months.

15. Always lock your classroom door if you will be away for more than a few minutes.

16. Food in your classroom should be kept in air tight containers.

17. Keep cleaning supplies in your room, locked away from the children. Never come in contact with any form of bodily fluid.

18. Shaving cream is a fun way to have the tables cleaned!

19. Keep your classroom keys separate from your home/car keys. Yikes!

20. You will spend your own money on things for your classroom. Write it off at tax time, keep clean receipts.

21. Always have crayons and coloring books no matter what age you teach.

22. Make your classroom warm, inviting, pleasant and safe.

23. Music is marvelous in so many ways! It calms, re-directs and signals transitions, and is just plain fun!

24. Purchase inexpensive games, puzzles, toys, etc.

25. Put your personality and style into your teaching and classroom.

26. Pencils can be projectiles!

27. Ignore profanity, vulgarity, etc. written on tables. Just clean it.

28. Avoid locking your door from the outside when you class is in session unless it is a lockdown.

29. You can refuse to allow people in your classroom if you have a good reason.

30. Truth always wins! Post positive quotes in your classroom.

31. Children learn best in a safe, orderly, clean and supportive environment.

32. Keep enough extra food and drink for your entire class. Microwave popcorn, sodas, cookies, etc. are good choices. You might need it for extended emergency days. You can also use it if you have a student that needs something to eat.

33. Write you name on all your possessions.

34. Keep a lost and found box.

35. Have regular class meetings.

36. Re-arrange the furniture every other month or so.

37. Keep air freshener on hand. You will be glad you have it the day they serve beans in the cafeteria! Trust me on this one!

38. Stand at the door as your class enters. Keeping an eye on the classroom and the hallway.

39. Routinely check your classroom for safety hazards.

40. Select durable items for your classroom. Children are hard on things, especially if they do not own them.

41. Have a "time out" area in your classroom.

42. Purchase extra office supplies. The secretaries will love you for making their job a little easier.

Your school and community

1. Don't allow others to bad mouth your school, even if they are right.

2. Develop a relationship with the custodian. They work hard and receive very little recognition.

3. The school secretary knows everything!

4. Volunteer to help at sporting events, dances, etc. It is part of your job and the students love to see you there.

5. Be true to your school! Display school posters, mascots, colors.

6. Join the PTA or PTSO even if you only make it to one meeting.

7. Water fountains harbor a billion germs, as well as table tops, door knobs, etc.

8. Involve the community whenever you can.

9. Beware of fundraisers. Things get lost, stolen and eaten!

10. Give whenever you have the opportunity.

11. Contribute to the beautification of the school and grounds.

12. Help in the office when you some spare time. You will learn a lot and develop an appreciation for the work they do.

13. Cameras are everywhere!

14. Cafeteria food is pretty much the same everywhere.

15. Before you decide to switch schools, do your homework. The grass is not always greener!

16. Join your schools Sunshine Club (co-workers contribute to a fund that celebrates birthdays and sends cards or gifts when someone experiences a death, birth, illness) or start one.

17. Report needed repairs. Be persistent. Maintenance prioritizes orders and are often overwhelmed. They will fix the problem but don't expect them to clean up after themselves.

18. Know your building. Request a map if you need to (keep one in your sub folder) or make one. Walk around. Look around. Ask questions.

19. Never plan an event/class in the gym, library, cafeteria, etc. without getting permission first. It is pushy and rude. You would be upset if it were your room.

20. Learn about the community surrounding your school.

21.   Learn about the community your students live in.

22.   Know who your community partners are and thank them for their help and support.

23.   Take advantage of teacher discounts!

Robert
Catlin
Jr.

58

What do you do?????

1. A student kisses you.-These types of issues depend on the age of the student, circumstances and intent. Strongly discourage the behavior and explain that it is inappropriate. Report and document the incident.

2. Your check stub in incorrect-After you double check, talk with the bookkeeper. It could be any number of reasons.

3. You need supplies-If you need a large amount, have a fundraiser. Ask the school secretary if you need a few basic office supplies. Talk with your principal if you need specific or specialty items. It never hurts to ask for donations!

4. A student threatens you with bodily harm-Contact the main office ASAP. Have them removed but don't show fear.

5. Your computer malfunctions-Contact your school or system computer expert. Follow proper procedures and be patient.

6. You and a co-worker cannot agree on an issue-If it will not affect your job, let it go. Otherwise work it out to the benefit of both of you even if you must consult a third party.

7. A student tells you that they want to die-Report it to guidance. They are trained to handle these types of issues. Talk to the student to obtain more information.

8. A student tells you someone has a weapon-Contact the principal ASAP.

9. A stranger enters your room-Ask them who they are and what they need. Then tell them that they must sign in at the main office. Protect the children.

10. A parent calls your principal to complain about something you did-Be honest. Explain the situation. Apologize if necessary.

11. A parent is unhappy with their child's grade-Double check your records, explain the reason for the grade, give the child a chance to bring the grade up. If it is solid, stand your ground.

12. You are accused of thief-Consider the source and/or reason. Don't over explain. Learn from the experience.

13. A child injures themselves in your class-Call the parent with a brief explanation. Fill out an accident/incident report.

14. 14.A child has several bad bruises-Ask about the bruises, contact guidance.

15. A child complains of abdominal and rectal pain-Ask a few questions to get a clearer picture of the cause. Send them to the restroom. If you suspect abuse, contact the principal.

16. Drugs fall out of a student pocket-Detain the student, contact the office ASAP.

17. A student hits you-Contact the office and SRO. Follow due process, file a complaint or press charges. See a doctor if needed.

18. A fight breaks out in your class-Command them to stop 3 times. Contact the office ASAP. Do not encourage other students to break it up. Intervene as a last resort.

19. A child is secretly video taping you-Explain the rules/laws of the infraction. Give the device to the principal.

20. You lose important paperwork-Backtrack. See if you can get replacements or retrieve it if it is on your computer.

21. A child lies and says you hit them-Collect written statements from witnesses. Do not talk to the child alone.

22. You miss an important meeting-Get notes from co-workers. If asked about it, have a reason, not an excuse.

23. You have wardrobe malfunction-Excuse yourself, fix the problem, let it go.

24. A co-worker yells at you-Remain calm. Walk away. Talk with them later.

25. You feel sick-Tell a student to get a co-worker to cover your class. Go home if you need to.

26. A child has a seizure-Call the office, keep the other children calm and out of the way, contact the parents.

27. Important information is accidently forwarded to the wrong person-Send a retraction.

28. A student throws a rock through your window-Notify the office, maintenance, and the parents.

29. A student cuts another students hair-Make sure the student understands the problem then apply appropriate discipline.

30. A student complains of sexual harassment-Have them write a summary of the incident report it to the principal.

31. Two co-workers are having sex at school-You have several choices: mind you own business, if you are friendly with one of them warn them of the consequences of their behavior, tell the principal.

32. You are asked a very personal question-Respectful decline to answer, answer, or tell them it is none of their business.

33. A co-worker has a nervous breakdown-Shield it from the children, get help.

34. You find unkind remarks about you on the desk-Clean it and forget it. At least they wrote it instead of saying it to your face.

35. A student has a nosebleed-Follow procedures for dealing with bodily fluids.

36. A student verbally abuses you-Avoid being drawn into the attack, have the student removed. If they cannot be removed, ignore them and contact the parents.

37. You are missing some supplies-Keep your eyes open, count supplies or assign supplies.

38. Your class is totally out of control-Consider the source of the problem (s), develop a game plan, get helpful advice and parental support.

39. A substitute leaves your room a wreck-File out a sub report and never get the sub again.

40. A guest speaker ask students for personal information-Tell them you cannot allow it without parental consent.

41. You are locked down-Reassure you class and let them know that you will take care of them.

42. A parent comes to school to spank their child-Suggest that they go to the office.

43. Two parents get in a public, heated argument-Try to de-escalate the situation and contact the office.

44. A student refused to leave your class-Call the office or SRO

45. A parent wants their child out of your class-Refer them to guidance. Let it go.

46. You are the target of gossip-Don't try to defend yourself. Don't try to investigate. Don't retaliate.

47. You are given more work than you can handle-Delegate. Ask for help. Prioritize. Learn to say "No".

48. A child wets or soils their pants-Call for the custodian. Let the child clean up and change clothes. Reassure them that they will be fine. Don't allow others to tease them.

49. A student tells you something of theirs was stolen-Get a good description of the item. Allow them to search the room and ask the class about it. If someone claims it, they need to provide witnesses.

50. A student skips your class-Notify the office

51. A student has frequent, unexcused absence-Send a letter to the parents explaining the school policy on absences.

52. A student refuses to do their work-Talk to them to find out why. There is always a reason.

53. A parent becomes physically aggressive with you-Defend yourself or retreat. Then, report the incident to SRO and principal.

54. A student touches themselves during class-Ignore it unless it becomes a problem.

55. You have a self-mutilator-Keep dangerous objects away. Contact guidance.

56. You have a selective mute-Give them time, encourage dialoge, don't push and show them a way to communicate.

57. A student walks out of class-Notify the office. You are responsible for that child.

58. You have a note passer-Give "the look" and tell them to put it away. If it continues, take the note, but never read it aloud.

59. You have a class bully-Set up a plan to end it that involves parents, co-workers and administration.

60. You have a tattletale-Discourage their behavior.

61. A student comes to class drunk-Contact the office ASAP

62. A co-worker flirts with you-If it is harmless, forget it. If it intensifies to the point of harassment, file a complaint.

63. A co-worker flirts with one of the students-Report it ASAP

64. A student tells you they don't want to go home-Find out why.

65. A student is passing out pills-Confiscate the pills, contact office.

66. Students are caught gambling-Refer to school policy. Contact parents.

67. A student tells you they are in a gang-Take note, but mind your own business.

68. Food fight!-Get help regaining order.

69. An animal gets in the building-Contact the custodian and keep the children away from the animal.

70. A student tells you they are a witch-Mind you own business and tell students to do the same.

71. A student draws a profane picture-Explain implications of the picture. Contact parents. Save the picture for future reference.

72. A student tells you their big brother takes drugs-Listen, avoid judgements, and warn student to not touch the drugs.

73. "Mr. Jones said I could"-Tell them to produce proof.

74. A student spits on you-Consider the situation. If the student is not special needs and the act was intentional, contact the office and parents.

75. Someone throws a pencil at you when your back is turned-Ask who threw it, if no one confesses, take away a class previlage.

76. A student is constantly up and down- Make an agreement that they can get up at appropriate times if they do not disrupt class.

77. A student cheats on a test-Failing grade or re-take depending on the circumstances.

78. A student talks loudly all the time-Suggest a hearing test or check the home situation.
79. A student doesn't answer to their name-Check their hearing and their name. You may be pronouncing it incorrectly or they might be used to a nickname.
80. You have a space invader!-Teach them about boundaries in a way that they will understand.
81. You have a teacher pleaser-Be glade but encourage them to tone it down.
82. A student is ill but you cannot reach a parent-Call everyone on the students contact list. Send them to the office if they are really sick.
83. You have a sarcastic smarty pants-Ignore them, literally, until they get the message. If they don't, begin issuing consequences. Pull them aside and warn with them.
84. A student always squints-Contact parents and suggests an eye exam.
85. A disfigured student is teased-Send the student on an errand while you talk to the class.
86. A student refuses to do their work-Find out why.
87. A co-worker borrows your supplies w/o permission-Get your supplies back and tell them where they can purchase their own.

88. A co-worker abruptly disrupts your class-If it isn't an emergency, ignore them or tell them to wait.

89. A parent wants to come to class with their child-Find out why and if it is for a good reason, welcome them. It could be a cautionary tale for the others.

90. You cannot account for all your students on a field-Get the others on the bus, but stop everything until you find the child.

91. One of your students passes away-If you cannot attend the funeral, send a card. Allow the other students time to grieve.

92. You are on the verge of punching a student!-Leave the room! Calm down. It is not worth it and you are the adult.

93. Someone has gas!-Open a window. Don't embarrass anyone. Remind the class that it is a normal, bodily function. But let the first student that ask to go to the restroom go!

94. You accidently use profanity-Apologize. We're all human.

95. You have a student with a potty mouth-Overlook it if it is not too bad or too frequent. Help them find replacement words.

96. A student brings a pet to school-Call a parent to come pick it up.

97. You feel terrible but have to work-Medicate yourself and ask co-workers for support.

98. Most of your class fails a test-Re-teach the lesson. They obviously didn't get it the first time.

99. You have a rodent!-Contact the custodian for glue traps. Don't tell the class.

100. You are contacted by the media-No comment!

101. A parent hates your principal-Mind your own business and shut your mouth.

102. A student deliberately breaks something-Contact parents. They might replace it, but don't count on it.

103. A student cannot keep their hands to themselves-Change their seat. Remind them of the consequences.

104. A student has a meltdown-Remove them from class to a place where they can calm down. Contact parents.

105. They're playing the choking game!-Contact parents, warn students of the dangers associated with the game, notify principal.

106. A student dresses too old for their age-Unless it is a distraction, mind your own business.

107. A student is too sexual for their age-Notify guidance.

108. A parent yells at you over the phone-Tell them you will continue the conversation when they calm down and are ready to talk. Hang up.

Final Words

So, there you have it, a 29 year collection of advice. It is, without a doubt, a daunting task. As I cruise the local bookstore, I cannot help but notice the number of books devoted to teachers concerning prayer. This leads me to the conclusion that one is called to teach. Prepare yourself for a career that will be anything but boring. The future is in your hands. You cannot become a doctor, lawyer, etc. without the help of a teacher.

The educational field is in need of not only good but dedicated teachers. Our nation faces a teacher shortage. No doubt due to the fact that teachers are under paid, over worked, and under constant criticism. Are there bad teachers? Unfortunately, yes. Some never learn how to teach, burn out due to the demands of the job, are not suited to work with children, or go into the profession for the wrong reason.

We live in a world that is increasing scary, especially for our children. We must teach them to survive and since they spent 7 hours a day at school, it only makes sense to begin in the classroom by educating them. As we partner with parents and the community, we can produce well-adjusted, intelligent, self-disciplined, responsible adults. Our future depends on it.

Printed in the United States
By Bookmasters